PLANET ANIMAL

POLAR BEAR lives in the lands of the Arctic. It also swims around the sea-ice.

Arctic Ocean

BACTRIAN CAMEL

ASIAN ELEPHANT

EUROPE

NORTH AMERICA

BLUE WHALE lives in all of the world's oceans.

GHARIAL

SOUTH AMERICA

Atlantic Ocean

AFRICA

Indian Ocean

Pacific Ocean

BENGAL TIGER

BLACK RHINOCEROS

LEATHERBACK TURTLE lives in many of the world's oceans.

GIANT PANDA

MOUNTAIN GORILLA

ASIA

Pacific Ocean

ORANG-UTAN

N
W ← → E
S

AUSTRALASIA

Southern Ocean

WANDERING ALBATROSS

PLANET ANIMAL

Our planet is home to thousands of different kinds of animals, but many are in danger of dying out, or becoming extinct. In *Planet Animal*, you'll travel the world to discover which animals are at risk. You'll also find out what we can do to stop these threatened, or endangered, animals disappearing forever.

Where endangered animals live

Look at this map of the world to find out where the animals shown in *Planet Animal* live.

ASIAN ELEPHANT
India, Sri Lanka, Indochina and parts of Indonesia

GIANT PANDA
Central-western and south-western China

BACTRIAN CAMEL
Eastern Asia, China and Mongolia

MOUNTAIN GORILLA
Central African countries of Uganda and Rwanda

BENGAL TIGER
Bangladesh, India, Nepal, Bhutan, Myanmar, Tibet

ORANG-UTAN
The islands of Sumatra and Borneo

BLACK RHINOCEROS
Eastern and central areas of Africa

POLAR BEAR
Greenland, Alaska, Canada, Svalbard, Franz-Josef Land

GHARIAL
Bhutan, Bangladesh, India, Myanmar, Pakistan, Nepal

WANDERING ALBATROSS
The land and skies of the Southern Ocean

The leatherback turtle and the blue whale swim great distances. They are found in many of the world's oceans.

LEATHERBACK TURTLE
Atlantic, Pacific, Indian and Southern oceans

BLUE WHALE
Atlantic, Pacific, Arctic, Southern and Indian oceans

ANIMALS IN DANGER!

Can you imagine a world without gorillas, tigers and polar bears? A world like this is much closer than you think. Many different types, or species, of animals may soon become extinct, or die out. Extinction is a natural process that has been happening for centuries, but it is now happening much more quickly and to many more species. People are the main problem because animals are being killed by man-made pollution, hunting and destruction of the wild places where they live. But if we all act now, we may be able to clean up our planet and save the animals for the future.

A PLACE TO LIVE

The most important threat to rare animals is the destruction of their natural home, or habitat.

⚠ **DANGER!** · People destroy habitats by cutting down forests, digging up grasslands and bulldozing coastlines to build houses, farms and factories.
· Rare animals bred in zoos and wildlife parks can't be released back into the wild if their habitat has been destroyed.

🌐 **HELP!** · Setting aside more nature reserves and wildlife parks will help to save the animals.
· Attracting tourists to nature reserves to see rare animals brings in money. This can stop local people from hunting the animals or destroying their habitat.

Huge areas of rainforest have been destroyed to build palm-oil plantations.

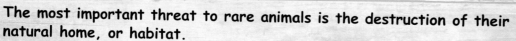

LATEST FIGURES...
SCIENTISTS BELIEVE THAT AT LEAST 8,000 ANIMAL SPECIES ARE IN DANGER OF BECOMING EXTINCT IN THE NEAR FUTURE.

CLIMATE CHANGE

Scientists think that the world will become much hotter. This is called global warming.

⚠️ **DANGER!** • If the Earth gets too hot, more animals could become extinct. The rise in temperature might cause droughts, famine, floods, hurricanes, heatwaves and wildfires. It could also lead to more ice-sheets and sea-ice melting away.

🌐 **HELP!** • Gases from factories and vehicles build up in the atmosphere and trap heat, creating a "greenhouse" effect. Developing alternative sources of energy that do not release "greenhouse gases" could help.

The polar bear's habitat is under threat because climate change is making the Arctic ice sheets melt.

PROTECTION FROM HUNTING

Poachers hunt endangered animals illegally, but rare animals can also be killed by accident.

⚠️ **DANGER!** • The fur and body parts of rare animals are used to make traditional medicines, tourist souvenirs and expensive clothes.
• Rare animals are captured illegally by traders to be sold as pets.
• At sea, endangered animals are trapped and killed accidentally on hooks or in nets intended for more common animals.

🌐 **HELP!** • Anti-poaching patrols in reserves or wildlife parks can help to protect animals from illegal hunting.
• Better enforcement of laws against the trade in endangered species could save animals, as could warning tourists against buying souvenirs made from rare animals.
• Developing safer fishing equipment and methods can prevent rare animals from being caught by mistake.

Rangers remove a rhino's horn. This makes it less likely to be killed by poachers.

A CLEANER WORLD

Conservationists clean up penguins and other sea birds caught in dangerous oil spills.

Animals are threatened by many different types of pollution. These include oil spills, poisonous chemicals, waste gases and the spread of deadly diseases.

⚠️ **DANGER!** • Oil spills from tanker accidents threaten animals both in the sea and on the coast.
• Gases from factories, vehicles and homes pollute the air we breathe. They are also causing the earth's climate to get warmer.
• Diseases spread by people as they move around the world may wipe out rare species.

🌐 **HELP!** • Tighter controls and safety checks on oil tankers can help to prevent accidents.
• New fuel sources and manufacturing methods could cut pollution.
• Research into finding new ways to fight diseases and to prevent them spreading will help reduce the risk to endangered animals.

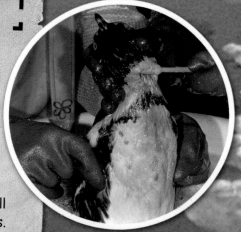

Disappearing tigers

Prowling silently through the jungle in search of prey, the mighty Bengal tiger is one of the most ferocious hunters. As the tiger creeps up on prey, its stripy orange-and-black fur blends in against the sun-bleached grasslands, muddy swamps and the dappled shade of leafy jungles. Then the tiger pounces. At each kill, a Bengal tiger can eat as much as 18 kg (40 lbs), which is enough meat to make 160 hamburgers! In the last 100 years, many types of tiger have become extinct. The Bengal tiger, which lives in Bangladesh, India and south-east Asia, is the most common species, but there are many problems to overcome if it is going to survive in the wild in the future.

WHAT BIG TEETH YOU HAVE!

A tiger has powerful jaws and four long, pointed front teeth, called canines. When the tiger bites the throat of its prey, it suffocates the captured animal. A bite to the neck kills the prey by breaking its spinal cord. The tiger uses its sharp cheek teeth to tear the meat off the prey's bones and to cut it into small pieces.

- FACT -
Bengal tiger cubs practise important survival skills by play-fighting together.

SUPREME HUNTER

A Bengal tiger's favourite food is wild deer. Tigers can't run as fast as the nimble deer, so they stalk them and wait until they are close before pouncing. The tiger crouches, with its head up, placing each foot on the ground. At the last moment, it rushes in for the kill. Tigers will eat any animals they can catch, including wild pigs, monkeys, fish and even baby elephants. The big cats rest in the shade by day and hunt mainly at night.

LATEST FIGURES...
SCIENTISTS ESTIMATE THERE ARE ABOUT 3,000 TO 5,000 TIGERS LEFT IN THE WILD, RANGING FROM SIBERIA TO INDIA AND SOUTH-EAST ASIA.

⚠️ TIGERS IN DANGER

🐾 Many Bengal tigers are killed illegally for their fur and body parts. Their bones and organs are used in traditional medicine.

🐾 When prey is scarce, tigers may attack farm animals. Local people kill the tigers to protect their livestock.

🐾 The Bengal tiger's habitat is being destroyed to make room for more villages and towns.

TIGER TOURISM

To make sure Bengal tigers survive, more protected areas are needed where they can hunt and live without the fear of poaching. Tourism helps the tigers by bringing in money to maintain these areas. Researchers take tourists on elephant safaris to show them how the tigers live in the wild.

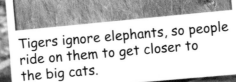

Tigers ignore elephants, so people ride on them to get closer to the big cats.

HOW BIG?

ADULT MALE:
length 2.7–3.1 m (8.9–10.2 ft)
weight 180–270 kg (397–595 lbs)

2 MONTHS OLD:
length 1 m (3.3 ft)
weight 7 kg (15.4 lbs)

DOMESTIC CAT:
length 70 cm (2.3 ft)
weight 3.5 kg (7.7 lbs)

Awesome albatross

If there were a competition for the best long-distance flier in the bird world, the wandering albatross would be the winner. Soaring through the air like huge, feathered gliders, albatrosses fly enormous distances for hours, or even days, without beating their wings. Their vast wing-span helps them glide over the Southern Ocean. Blown along by the wind and air currents, they fly thousands of kilometres in search of food. Wanderers are the largest of all the albatross species, spending almost all their lives at sea. They return to the land where they were born only to mate and raise their chicks.

Albatrosses are in real danger of becoming extinct. At the moment, large numbers of these birds are killed at sea near fishing boats with lines and hooks. But there are ways we can help to save them...

HOW BIG?

ADULT WANDERING ALBATROSS:
wing-span 3.3 m (10.8 ft)
weight 8 kg (18 lbs)

ADULT COMMON GULL:
wing-span 1.1–1.3 m (3.6 ft–4.3 ft)
weight 300–500 g (0.7–1.1 lbs)

HANG-GLIDER:
wing-span 10 m (33 ft)
weight 33 kg (73 lbs)

LATEST FIGURES...
SCIENTISTS ESTIMATE THAT THERE ARE ABOUT 9,000 PAIRS OF WANDERING ALBATROSSES LEFT IN THE SOUTHERN OCEAN.

TAKE-OFF!

Albatrosses are graceful fliers, but they are clumsy when they take-off and land. They are too heavy to leap into the air to take-off and their wings are too long. Instead, they run downhill with their wings outstretched until they are moving fast enough to lift off into the air. To land, albatrosses spread out their tails and webbed feet to help them "brake". If they are going too fast when they stop on dry land, they topple forwards, beak first, in an untidy heap!

⚠️ ALBATROSSES IN DANGER

Hungry albatrosses try to steal squid from the bait hooks on long lines that trail from the backs of fishing boats. Often, their beaks get caught on the hooks. They are pulled underwater and drown.

Lost hooks and lines stuck in floating bait can choke the birds.

Large numbers of albatrosses drown when they get caught in fishing nets.

BILLS AND FEEDING

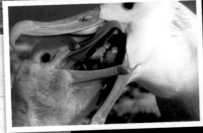

The hooked bill of an albatross has sharp edges and is perfect for grabbing slippery fish and squid. Wandering albatrosses dip their heads under the surface to catch food and dive under the water to chase their prey. They also scavenge for dead animals floating on the sea. Albatross chicks take food directly from an adult's bill.

SAVE THE ALBATROSS!

Here are a few ways to save albatrosses from being killed on long-line hooks:
• banning fishing in areas where seabirds gather to feed
• setting fishing lines underwater
• using special bird-scaring lines fitted with cones and streamers that frighten the birds away.

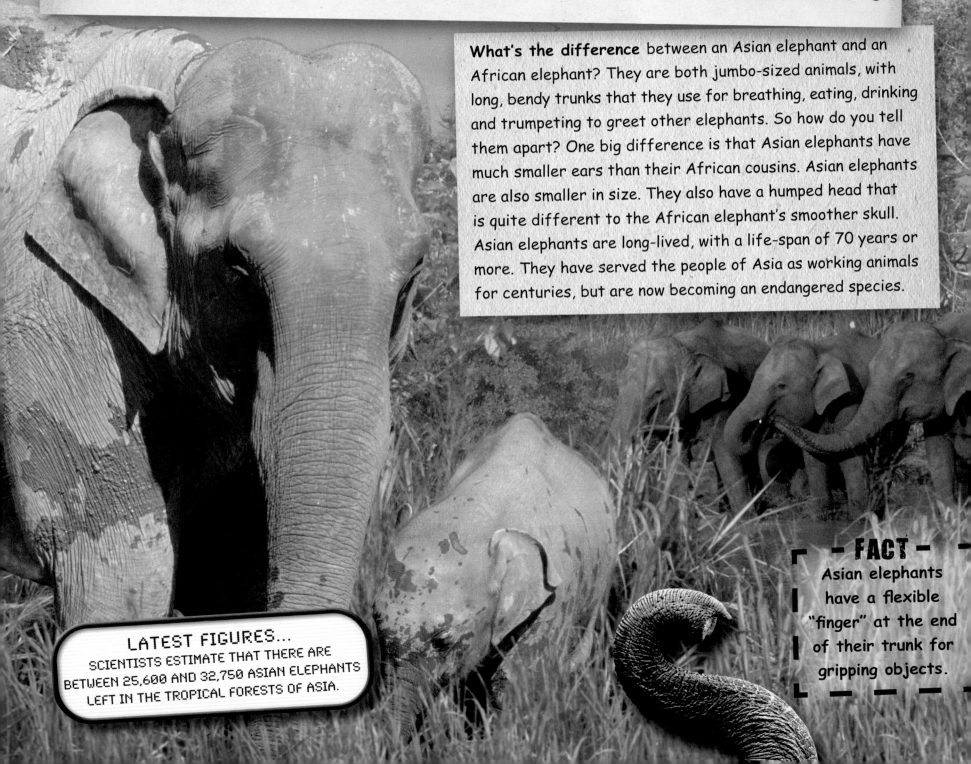

ASIAN ELEPHANT ALERT!

What's the difference between an Asian elephant and an African elephant? They are both jumbo-sized animals, with long, bendy trunks that they use for breathing, eating, drinking and trumpeting to greet other elephants. So how do you tell them apart? One big difference is that Asian elephants have much smaller ears than their African cousins. Asian elephants are also smaller in size. They also have a humped head that is quite different to the African elephant's smoother skull. Asian elephants are long-lived, with a life-span of 70 years or more. They have served the people of Asia as working animals for centuries, but are now becoming an endangered species.

LATEST FIGURES...
SCIENTISTS ESTIMATE THAT THERE ARE BETWEEN 25,600 AND 32,750 ASIAN ELEPHANTS LEFT IN THE TROPICAL FORESTS OF ASIA.

- FACT -
Asian elephants have a flexible "finger" at the end of their trunk for gripping objects.

ELEPHANT GOD

In the Hindu religion, Ganesh, the god of wisdom, has the head of an elephant. He got his head when his father, Siva, cut off Ganesh's own head in a terrible rage. Ganesh's mother, the goddess Parvati, was so angry that she forced Siva to give her son the head of the first animal to pass by. Hindus believe Ganesh provides good luck for important tasks, such as exams or business deals.

⚠️ ELEPHANTS IN DANGER

🐘 Asia's rapidly growing human population has put pressure on the elephants. Local people are cutting down more and more forest for timber and farming, leaving the elephants homeless.

🐘 Poachers are a major threat to elephants. They kill the animals to sell their tusks, meat and thick hide.

🐘 Elephants have gigantic appetites. This causes conflict with farmers, who drive elephants away to stop them raiding crops.

🐘 When elephants roam looking for food, their paths may be blocked by roads or towns, so they end up in areas where food is scarce.

HOW BIG?

ADULT MALE:
height 2–3 m (6.6–9.8 ft)
weight 2–5 tonnes
(2.2–5.5 tons)

NEWBORN BABY:
height 1 m (3.3 ft)
weight 50–150 kg
(110–331 lbs)

SCHOOL BUS:
height 3 m (9.8 ft)
weight 12 tonnes
(13.2 tons)

TEETH AND TUSKS

An elephant has four huge teeth inside its mouth, two on each side. It uses them for grinding down leaves, branches and bark. In the top jaw, there may also be two front teeth called tusks, which grow outside the mouth. Only some male Asian elephants have tusks. Females have small tusks, called tushes, that grow slowly and often don't show.

Each back tooth weighs as much as a house brick!

🛟 GOOD FOR THE PLANET

Elephants play a vital role in their habitat. Their dung provides the soil with nutrients that help plants to grow. Elephants sometimes dig wells to get to water below the ground, which also enables other animals to drink. And working elephants don't create pollution, unlike petrol-burning tractors and trucks!

PANDAS IN PERIL

It's difficult to find a giant panda in the wild! These cute-looking creatures are very shy and they try to stay away from people. Pandas live in dense bamboo forests in the mountains of China. The weather in the forests is misty and cold, but the pandas are kept warm by their thick fur coats. The Chinese name for the giant panda, *da xiong mao*, means "great bear cat". Scientists think these rare black-and-white animals are related to bears. Pandas are gentle creatures, but they are fiercely protective of their young. They spend most of their time looking for and eating bamboo, a kind of giant grass with thick, crunchy stems.

SNOW FUN

In the wild, pandas live by themselves and rarely meet up except to mate. But in zoos and breeding centres they enjoy playing together in the snow.

- FACT -

Pandas are good at climbing trees. They also like to snuggle up in hollow trees to sleep.

VEGGIE BEAR

Giant pandas are vegetarians with a special diet. They eat the leaves, stems and shoots of about 30 different types of bamboo. Bamboo contains only small amounts of goodness, so giant pandas have to eat an awful lot of it to stay healthy. The animals munch their way through half their body weight of bamboo every day. To hold the bamboo stems, the pandas have a tough pad on their palm, below their first finger. This extra "thumb" is actually an enlarged wrist bone.

HOW BIG

ADULT MALE:
height 1.5 m (4.9 ft)
weight 80 kg (176 lbs)

6 MONTHS OLD:
height 1 m (3.3 ft)
weight 13 kg (28.7 lbs)

4-YEAR-OLD BOY:
height 1 m (3.3 ft)
weight 17 kg (37.5 lbs)

⚠ PANDAS IN DANGER

🐾 Giant pandas are at risk from the destruction of their forest. Local people need the land for farming and timber and to build roads.

🐾 Even though pandas are a protected species, gangs kill them for their valuable fur.

🐾 Pandas die when they are caught accidentally in deer and bear traps.

🐾 Pandas do not produce many cubs, so panda populations stay low.

🐾 Sometimes all the bamboo in a feeding area dies off. This leaves the pandas at risk from starvation.

BREEDING PANDAS

Experts at the Wolong Breeding Centre in China have learned how to breed pandas successfully. Cubs weigh only as much as an apple when they are born! In 2006, the first of the pandas raised at the centre was set free. The plan is to release more pandas into the wild to boost the population.

LATEST FIGURES...

SCIENTISTS ESTIMATE THAT THERE ARE ABOUT 1,600 GIANT PANDAS LEFT IN THE FORESTS OF SOUTH-WESTERN CHINA.

THE LAST GHARIALS

With its strange, **pointy snout**, the gharial is the oddest looking member of the crocodile and alligator family. It lives in the fast-moving rivers of northern India, Nepal, Pakistan, Bangladesh, Bhutan and Burma (Myanmar), where it hunts for fish with its long, narrow jaws. A gharial has over 100 needle-like teeth, which are perfect for catching its slippery prey. Gharials are not dangerous to people because their jaws are too thin and fragile to attack large animals. With their powerful tails and strong webbed feet, gharials are fast and graceful swimmers. At one time, gharials lived in almost every river in northern India, but because of hunting and pollution, they are now nearly extinct.

- FACT -
If one of a gharial's teeth falls out, a brand-new tooth grows to replace it.

"POTTY" NOSE

Gharials are named after the unusual, pot-shaped lump on the male's snout. The word *ghara* is the Indian word for a large clay pot. The male gharial uses his swollen nose lump to blow bubbles in the water as part of his courtship ritual!

⚠ GHARIALS IN DANGER

- The gharial's habitat is threatened by schemes to divert water from their rivers to farmers' fields.

- Local people harvest gharial eggs for food. They hunt the adult gharials to use their body parts in traditional medicines.

- Since 1991, the money spent trying to breed gharials in captivity has been cut. As a result, the number of gharials is still going down.

EGGS AND NESTS

In the wild, very few baby gharials survive to become adults. To help more babies grow up safely, scientists collect gharial eggs from nests on river-banks and raise the young in a safe enclosure. When these gharials have grown big enough to cope with most dangers, they are set free into the river.

HOW BIG?

ADULT MALE:
length **4–6 m (13–20 ft)**
weight **159 kg (350 lbs)**

NEWBORN GHARIAL:
length **20 cm (8 in)**
weight **60 g (0.1 lbs)**

DIVER:
height **1.8 m (5.9 ft)**
weight **70 kg (154 lbs)**

FISHY SNACKS

Young gharials catch small creatures, such as insects and frogs, but the adults eat mainly fish. They stay still underwater, waiting for a fish to swim past, then swipe their long snout sideways to snap it up. Their pointed teeth are no good for chewing food, so the gharials swallow their meals in one big gulp.

Camel crisis

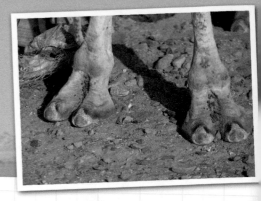

HOW BIG?

ADULT MALE:
height **2 m (6.6 ft)**
weight **700 kg (1,543 lbs)**

1 YEAR OLD:
height **1 m (3.3 ft)**
weight **150 kg (331 lbs)**

HORSE:
height **1.5 m (4.9 ft)**
weight **500 kg (1,102 lbs)**

How would you like to live in a place that used to be underwater? Well, the Bactrian camel loves it! This wild camel is only found in the Gobi Desert, which was once a large inland sea. Today there is hardly enough water left to drink and it rains only every two or three years.
A Bactrian camel is specially designed to live in the desert. It can travel long distances in search of food and can survive for months without water. The two humps on its back even act as emergency lunch-boxes. These humps are filled with fat, which gives the camel enough energy to survive until its next proper meal of grass and plants. Even though wild Bactrian camels are tough enough to live in the desert, they are still in danger. Scientists think the camels could die out within 30 years.

FLAT FEET

Camels have specially shaped feet that let them walk across the soft desert sand without sinking. A camel's feet are wide and flat, which means that its weight is spread out evenly. Each foot has only two toes, but the foot bones actually stretch out sideways when it walks. A patch of skin under the toes helps make the foot even wider.

- FACT -

Camels can close their nostrils tightly to keep out sand.

⚠ CAMELS IN DANGER

- Even though China used to test nuclear weapons in the Gobi Desert, Bactrian camels managed to survive the dangerous explosions.

- There is very little water in the desert and farmers sometimes kill camels because they want only their cattle to drink it.

- For hundreds of years, wild Bactrian camels have been hunted by humans for their meat and fur.

- Unless we do something right now to save the camels, there could be fewer than 200 left by the year 2033.

FUR COAT

Bactrian camels live in deserts, where winter temperatures fall way below freezing. In the autumn, they grow an extra-thick coat to keep them warm through the chilly winter months. Then, when temperatures rise, the following spring they moult, or shed, this woolly hair. The camels' hair moults in long, ragged patches.

SAVE THE CAMEL!

Many types of camels are hunted for sport or have died out because the places where they live have been taken over by humans. The wild camels that survive now live in nature reserves, such as The Great Gobi Reserve in Mongolia or the Lop Nur Wild Camel Reserve in China, but lots more of these reserves are needed.

People kill wild Bactrian camels to stop them eating the scarce food needed by working camels.

LATEST FIGURES...
SCIENTISTS ESTIMATE THAT THERE ARE ONLY ABOUT 950 WILD BACTRIAN CAMELS LEFT IN THE DESERTS OF CHINA AND MONGOLIA.

GENTLE GIANTS

Bamboo and thistles may not sound like a tasty snack to a human, but to a mountain gorilla they are the perfect food for breakfast, lunch and dinner! One of our closest living relatives, the shy mountain gorilla is the largest and rarest of the great apes. These intelligent, human-like animals have grasping hands and feet. Mountain gorillas eat mostly plants. As well as bamboo and thistles, they also enjoy celery, nettles, vines, fruit, stems, roots and bark. They make their home in the dense rainforests of central Africa, living in small family groups of about eight to 10 apes, led by an adult male. The male is called a silverback because it has silvery hair on its back. Scientists spend a lot of time observing mountain gorillas. By bringing attention to the problems the animals face, scientists hope to save these gentle giants and prevent the destruction of their forest home.

LATEST FIGURES...
SCIENTISTS ESTIMATE THAT THERE ARE ABOUT 700 MOUNTAIN GORILLAS LEFT IN THE FORESTS OF CENTRAL AFRICA.

NOSE PRINTS
A gorilla's nose is its most distinctive feature. Like human fingerprints, no two noses are exactly alike. Scientists working on conservation projects identify individual animals by the unique shape of their noses and nostrils.

HOW BIG?

ADULT MALE:
height 1.7 m (5.6 ft)
weight 150 kg (331 lbs)

I YEAR OLD:
height 0.4 m (1.3 ft)
weight 25 kg (55.1 lbs)

TOURIST:
height 1.8 m (5.9 ft)
weight 65 kg (143 lbs)

LUNCHTIME NAP
In the middle of the day, the gorillas build day nests on the ground and rest for a while to digest their food and socialize. They sunbathe, althou it is usually misty and rainy in t mountain forests. The gorillas' thick fur keeps them dry and warm.

⚠️ GORILLAS IN DANGER

- Wars disrupt the forest and threaten the gorillas' safety.

- Their forests are being destroyed by people who need to farm the land to survive and who fell forest trees for firewood.

- Gorillas are killed illegally for food, or their body parts are sold as souvenirs or for use in traditional medicines.

- People pass on disease because the gorillas are so similar to humans. Gorillas have little or no resistance to human illnesses.

- Many baby gorillas die of diseases and nearly half of all gorillas die before growing up into adults. If a baby does survive, it may live for 35 to 45 years.

THUMBS

Gorillas can pick up small and delicate objects without breaking them because their thumbs easily touch, or oppose, each of their fingers. This is called having an opposable thumb. Humans have opposable thumbs, too. A gorilla has bigger hands than we do, with fingers as thick as bananas! Like humans, gorillas have fingertip ridges to help grip slippery objects.

A gorilla fingerprint

Make your fingerprint in the space above

HELP AT HAND

Tourists pay a lot of money to visit mountain gorillas in the wild. The tourists' visits have to be carefully controlled to make sure the gorillas are not disturbed too much. Money from tourism helps to protect the gorillas' habitat. It also helps to fund and maintain facilities for the local people, such as fresh water supplies.

Saving the turtles

Sea turtles have lived on Earth for millions of years, since the days of their reptile relatives, the dinosaurs. Leatherback turtles are different from other sea turtles because they have a soft, leathery shell instead of a hard, bony one. Leatherbacks travel huge distances across the world's oceans, "flying" underwater using their powerful front flippers. They can dive to the dark, freezing-cold ocean depths in search of food, holding their breath for up to a half an hour before they have to come up for air. Nearly all sea turtle species are endangered, but the leatherbacks are most at risk because of the threat from pollution, litter and the destruction of their nesting areas.

JELLY FOR TEA

A leatherback's favourite food is jellyfish. The turtle has no teeth, so it catches and holds its slippery prey using its beak-like jaws. Special backward-pointing spines in the turtle's throat stop the jellyfish from escaping. Unfortunately, floating plastic bags look like jellyfish. The turtles often eat the bags, which can kill them.

⚠ TURTLES IN DANGER

- Turtles get tangled up in fishing gear and litter drifting in the ocean. Eventually they drown.
- Pollution damages turtle feeding areas, such as coral reefs. It also poisons the turtles.
- Boats and jet-skis crash into swimming turtles.
- Hotel complexes destroy turtle beaches, and careless tourists disturb the females as they try to lay their eggs.
- Local people catch turtles and collect their eggs to sell for food.

- FACT -
Leatherbacks attract suckerfish, which hitch a ride on the turtles as they swim.

SAFE HAVEN

On some beaches where leatherback turtles lay their eggs, conservation groups have created protected areas where the eggs can hatch in safety. Female leatherbacks may lay 60–120 eggs in a nest in about two hours. When the babies hatch from the eggs, people carry them down to the sea. This helps the turtles survive, as it stops them from being attacked by other animals on the way to the water.

TRACKING THE TURTLES

By learning more about leatherbacks, we can find new ways to protect them. When a nesting female crawls ashore, scientists attach a tag to the turtle's back. The tag doesn't hurt the turtle and carries a radio transmitter. This sends a signal that the scientists can track to find out where the turtle swims on its travels.

EGG LAYERS

As soon as a female leatherback turtle has laid her eggs, she heads back to the sea, leaving the baby turtles to develop on their own in the warmth of their sandy nest. If the temperature in the nest is high, more females hatch out, while lower temperatures produce more males.

A baby turtle takes about two months to develop. All the baby turtles in the nest tend to hatch out at roughly the same time. They usually hatch under the cover of darkness and race down to the sea, trying to avoid the many predators, such as seabirds, crabs, dogs and raccoons.

LATEST FIGURES...
SCIENTISTS ESTIMATE THAT THERE ARE ABOUT 25,000 NESTING FEMALE LEATHERBACK TURTLES LEFT IN THE WORLD'S OCEANS.

HOW BIG?

ADULT FEMALE:
length 1.5–2.5 m (5–8 ft)
weight 250–900 kg
(551–1,984 lbs)

NEWBORN TURTLE:
length 5 cm (2 in)
weight 35 g (0.07 lbs)

SURFER:
height 1.8 m (6 ft)
weight 70 kg (154 lbs)

The Ice Bear

Imagine living in a place that's colder than the inside of a freezer. At the top of the world, the frozen Arctic Ocean is one of the chilliest places on earth. But to polar bears, it's home. Sometimes called ice bears, these huge, powerful creatures feed mainly on the seals that they catch on the ice. Polar bears are most active at night. Usually they hunt and feed alone, except during the mating season. They also have webbed feet, which make them excellent swimmers.

 ⚠ **BEARS IN DANGER**

🐾 As well as global warming, the polar bear's habitat is threatened by mining and drilling for oil and gas.

🐾 Over-hunting of polar bears for sport could reduce their numbers in the future.

🐾 Pollution from factories is creating long-term problems for polar bears' health and is shortening their life-span.

UNDERWATER

HOW BIG

ADULT FEMALE:
height 1.5m (5 ft)
weight 200 kg (lbs)

6 MONTHS OLD:
height 0.4 m (1.3 ft)
weight 25 kg (55.1 lbs)

ARCTIC SCIENTIST:
height 1.8 m (5.9 ft)
weight 85 kg (187 lbs)

SNOW PAWS

A polar bear's enormous paws work like snowshoes. They help to spread out the bear's great weight and stop it sinking through ice or snow. The underside of the paws are rough and hairy, providing extra grip. Thick, curved claws work like the spikes on running shoes, preventing the bear from slipping.

SAVE THE POLAR BEAR!
HOW YOU CAN HELP

At school, ask your teacher about the organizations that are trying to help save the polar bears and how you can find out more about them. You can show your support for the important work these organizations are doing by writing them a letter like the one shown here.

Dear Friends of the Polar Bear,

I think that polar bears are amazing animals. I am very worried that they may become extinct one day, so I am glad that your organization is trying to do something to help them before it is too late.

I read an article in a newspaper which said that pollution and hunting are threatening the polar bears' future. It also said that by the year 2080, the Earth will have become so warm that the sea-ice where the bears feed on seals may disappear completely. I was very upset when I read about this, because if the bears can't find food, they all could die out! Let's hope that by doing something now we can stop this from happening.

Please keep up the good work you are doing. Even small changes can make a big difference!

Thank you for taking the time to read this letter.

From...

LATEST FIGURES...
ACCORDING TO A 2006 SURVEY, SCIENTISTS ESTIMATE THAT THERE ARE BETWEEN 20,000 AND 25,000 POLAR BEARS LEFT IN THE ARCTIC.

- FACT -
Usually, there are two cubs in a polar bear's litter.

Polar bears have two layers of fur and a layer of blubber under the skin to keep them warm.

SEAL MEALS

A polar bear's sense of smell is so powerful it can sniff out a seal under the ice from up to a kilometre (0.6 miles) away. Bears have to wait for hours, or even days, beside a seal's breathing hole. When the seal appears, one swipe of the bear's massive paw and a bite at the back of the skull are enough to make the kill. Then the bear digs its curved claws into the seal and heaves the body out of the water onto the ice. After feeding, a polar bear will spend up to 15 minutes cleaning its fur. It does this because wet and dirty fur will not keep the bear warm.

SNOW CAVES

When fierce winds blow on bitterly cold days, polar bears dig out shelters in snow banks and curl up into a tight ball until the storm is over. Winter temperatures in the Arctic drop to -40° F (-40° C) and stay that way for days or even weeks.

Rare Rhinos

If a rhino visited the doctor for a check-up it would do very well in its hearing test. Their ears can point in any direction, so they can hear a sound no matter which direction it is coming from. Rhinos also have a good sense of smell. If you tried to sneak up on a rhino it would hear or smell you before it saw you. Rhinos live in the grasslands of Africa and Asia. There are five different species, all of which are endangered. The black rhino, which lives in Africa, is the second most common rhino. Like all rhinos, it has a huge head and a massive body.

Rhinos are one of the few giant plant-eaters to survive from the ancient past. They look at bit like dinosaurs, but they are not related to these extinct reptiles.

- FACT -

The word "rhinoceros" means "nose horn" in Greek.

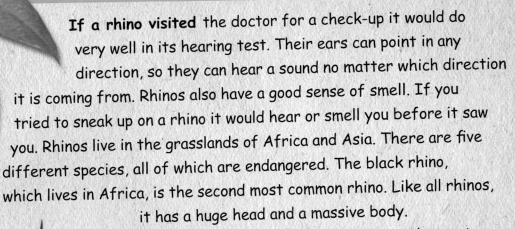

MUD BATH

A black rhino may have thick, tough skin but it can still get sunburnt! Instead of using sunscreen, African rhinos like to roll around in muddy water. This covers their skin in a thick layer of mud, which protects them from the hot sun and biting insects. The wet mud also helps the rhino to cool down in the heat of the day. Black rhinos get their name from the dark-coloured mud. They actually have grey skin but look black after a mud bath.

ON THE MOVE

One way to increase the amount of rhinos in the world is to keep a group of them in a protected area until they grow in numbers. Then some of the group can be airlifted by helicopter to other safe places where there are no rhinos at all. This means that the rhinos are not all living in the same place, which could be dangerous if there was a natural disaster such as a flood.

RHINO SPECS.

There are five species of rhino in the world, all of which are endangered.

BLACK RHINO
WHERE FROM:
Africa
NO. LEFT IN WILD
3,500

INDIAN RHINO
WHERE FROM:
India and Nepal
NO. LEFT IN WILD
2,500+

SUMATRAN RHINO
WHERE FROM:
Sumatra
NO. LEFT IN WILD
300

JAVAN RHINO
WHERE FROM:
Java and Vietnam
NO. LEFT IN WILD
50-70

WHITE RHINO
WHERE FROM:
Africa
NO. LEFT IN WILD
15,000+

HOW BIG?

ADULT MALE:
height 1.6 m (5.2 ft)
weight 1.4 tonnes
(1.5 tons)

1 YEAR OLD:
height 1 m (3.3 ft)
weight 0.6 tonne
(0.7 ton)

SMALL CAR:
height 1.4 m (4.6 ft)
weight 1 tonne
(1.1 tons)

⚠ RHINOS IN DANGER

The greatest threat to the rhinos' survival is the demand for their horns, which are ground up and used in traditional medicines in eastern Asia. The horns are also used to make dagger handles in the country of Yemen in the Middle East.

Since 1980, the trade in rhino horn has been banned, but rhinos are still killed illegally by poachers.

Habitat destruction by people needing to build homes and farms also threatens rhinos, especially in Asia.

REMOVING RHINO HORNS

To stop the rhino from becoming extinct, stronger enforcement of the law against trading in rhino horn is essential. By removing rhinos' valuable horns, conservationists try to protect the animals by making them less of a target for poachers. Reserves for all rhinos, with protection against poachers, are urgently needed.

LATEST FIGURES...
SCIENTISTS ESTIMATE THAT THERE ARE ABOUT 21,000 RHINOS LEFT IN THE GRASSLANDS AND FORESTS OF AFRICA AND ASIA.

Vanishing whales

▲ HUMPBACK WHALE
length: 14 m (46 ft)
Humpback whales are the acrobats of the ocean. They can leap up into the air and slap the water with their tails.

▲ BELUGA WHALE
length: 4 m (13 ft)
Beluga whales have a small, stout body, tiny eyes and a mouth that's full of teeth.

▸ NORTHERN RIGHT WHALE
length: 18 m (59 ft)
Northern right whales have two blow-holes and were named by whalers who thought they were the "right" whales to hunt.

▲ FIN WHALE
length: 23 m (75 ft)
After the blue whale, the fin whale is the largest animal on Earth. It is so fast that it's called the "greyhound of the sea".

▲ BLUE WHALE
length: 29.5 m (97 ft)
The blue whale is the largest animal on the Earth. It is as big as a jumbo jet and can eat 7 tonnes (7.7 tons) of food per day.

The blue whale is probably the largest animal ever to have lived on the Earth. Its heart is the same size as a small car and there's room for about 50 people to stand on its tongue! Like all whales, blue whales are warm-blooded and breathe air into their huge lungs through large blow-holes. Powerful back muscles and wide tail flukes help it to race through the water. Blue whales live in every ocean in the world. Unlike a sea, which is partly or fully surrounded by land, an ocean is a huge, unenclosed body of water. Whales spend a lot of time in the cool waters near the North and South Poles where there is plenty of food for them to eat. When winter arrives at the poles and the water starts to get very cold, the blue whales begin a long journey called a migration. The whales swim to warmer waters, where they mate and give birth to calves.

⚠ WHALES IN DANGER

- Pollution of the oceans by oil spills and poisonous chemicals endangers many whale species.

- The blue whale, the fin whale, the humpback whale, the beluga whale and the northern right whale are all under threat from hunting and pollution.

- For centuries, the Inuit people of the Arctic have hunted whales for their blubber and meat. The Inuits want to carry on hunting because it is a traditional part of their culture. Whale meat is also a major part of their diet.

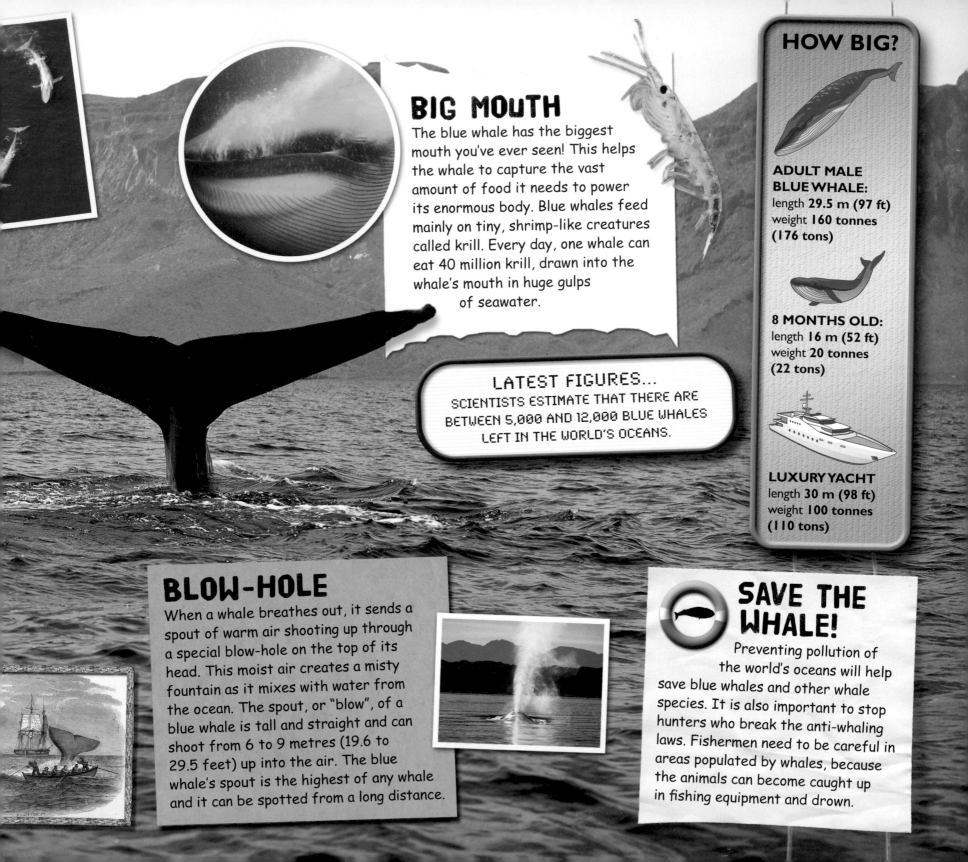

BIG MOUTH

The blue whale has the biggest mouth you've ever seen! This helps the whale to capture the vast amount of food it needs to power its enormous body. Blue whales feed mainly on tiny, shrimp-like creatures called krill. Every day, one whale can eat 40 million krill, drawn into the whale's mouth in huge gulps of seawater.

LATEST FIGURES...

SCIENTISTS ESTIMATE THAT THERE ARE BETWEEN 5,000 AND 12,000 BLUE WHALES LEFT IN THE WORLD'S OCEANS.

HOW BIG?

ADULT MALE BLUE WHALE:
length **29.5 m (97 ft)**
weight **160 tonnes (176 tons)**

8 MONTHS OLD:
length **16 m (52 ft)**
weight **20 tonnes (22 tons)**

LUXURY YACHT
length **30 m (98 ft)**
weight **100 tonnes (110 tons)**

BLOW-HOLE

When a whale breathes out, it sends a spout of warm air shooting up through a special blow-hole on the top of its head. This moist air creates a misty fountain as it mixes with water from the ocean. The spout, or "blow", of a blue whale is tall and straight and can shoot from 6 to 9 metres (19.6 to 29.5 feet) up into the air. The blue whale's spout is the highest of any whale and it can be spotted from a long distance.

SAVE THE WHALE!

Preventing pollution of the world's oceans will help save blue whales and other whale species. It is also important to stop hunters who break the anti-whaling laws. Fishermen need to be careful in areas populated by whales, because the animals can become caught up in fishing equipment and drown.

Red apes in danger

What do **orang-utans** do when it rains? They make umbrellas, of course! The intelligent apes pick up leaves and use them to keep the water off. Orang-utans live in rainforests on the south-east Asian islands of Borneo and Sumatra. They spend most of their time in the trees looking for fruit and seeds to eat. Orang-utans have good memories, which help them remember the best places to find food. People are destroying the orang-utans' natural habitat very quickly. Soon, they may only live in zoos and research centres.

HOW BIG?

ADULT MALE:
height 1.7 m (5.6 ft)
weight 120 kg (265 lbs)

1 YEAR OLD:
height 0.8 m (2.6 ft)
weight 40 kg (88 lbs)

GYMNAST:
height 1.6 m (5.2 ft)
weight 55 kg (121 lbs)

USING TOOLS

Like humans, orang-utans use tools to make their lives easier. First, they break off a branch and strip it of leaves. Then they use it as a stick to poke at termite nests, or even to scoop out honey from beehives.

LATEST FIGURES...
SCIENTISTS NOW ESTIMATE THAT THERE ARE ONLY BETWEEN 20,000 AND 30,000 ORANG-UTANS LEFT IN THE FORESTS OF BORNEO AND SUMATRA.

THE HIGH LIFE

Orang-utans are completely at home in the trees. Swinging effortlessly from tree to tree on their long arms, they have a powerful grip that lets them dangle from just one hand or foot. Their long fingers and toes curl around branches to give them a firm hold. Orang-utans hardly ever come down to the ground. It is easier to stay up in the trees where there is lots of food!

DONT MESS WITH ME!

Male orang-utans have fatty cheek pads that make them look bigger and scarier than they really are. They also roar loudly to warn other males to keep out of their patch of forest. These "long calls" mean that dangerous fights can be avoided.

FACT
The name "orang-utan" comes from the Malay words meaning "man of the forest".

⚠ ORANG-UTANS IN DANGER

✋ Huge areas of the orang-utans' rainforests are being cut down. Palm oil trees are planted, which produce an oil that is used to make fuels that cause less pollution. This is good for the environment, but it means that the orang-utans' habitat is being destroyed.

✋ The owners of palm-oil plantations kill the orang-utans because the hungry apes eat the young palm-oil plants.

✋ Each year, many orang-utans are captured illegally by animal traders. They are smuggled overseas and sold as pets.

SAVE THE ORANGUTAN!

Conservationists rescue orphaned baby orang-utans and raise them at special centres. These centres have tree platforms to recreate the orang-utans' natural habitat. Ideally, they would eventually be released into the wild. But today, this is impossible because there is no rainforest left where they are safe.

PLANET ANIMAL FUN QUIZ

Find out if you're an animal expert! The answers can be found in the pages of *Planet Animal* or in the box at the bottom of the opposite page.

TRUE OR FALSE?

Test your animal knowledge with these tricky true or false questions.

1. The gharial has 80 teeth in its very long jaws.

2. Pandas spend most of their time looking for or eating nettles.

3. Rhinos have a very poor sense of smell.

4. A polar bear's feet are like spiked running shoes.

5. Female gorillas are called silverbacks.

6. A tiger's fur is spotted for camouflage in the long grass.

GUESS WHO?

Can you identify these animals? The clues under each picture will give you helpful hints.

1. King of the swingers

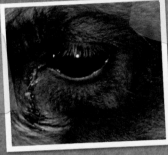

2. Desert dweller

3. Gentle vegetarian

4. Hidden hunter

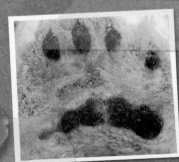

5. Big in the north

6. Bamboo eater

BRAIN-TEASERS

These questions will test your knowledge of endangered animals to the limit. Are you ready for the challenge?

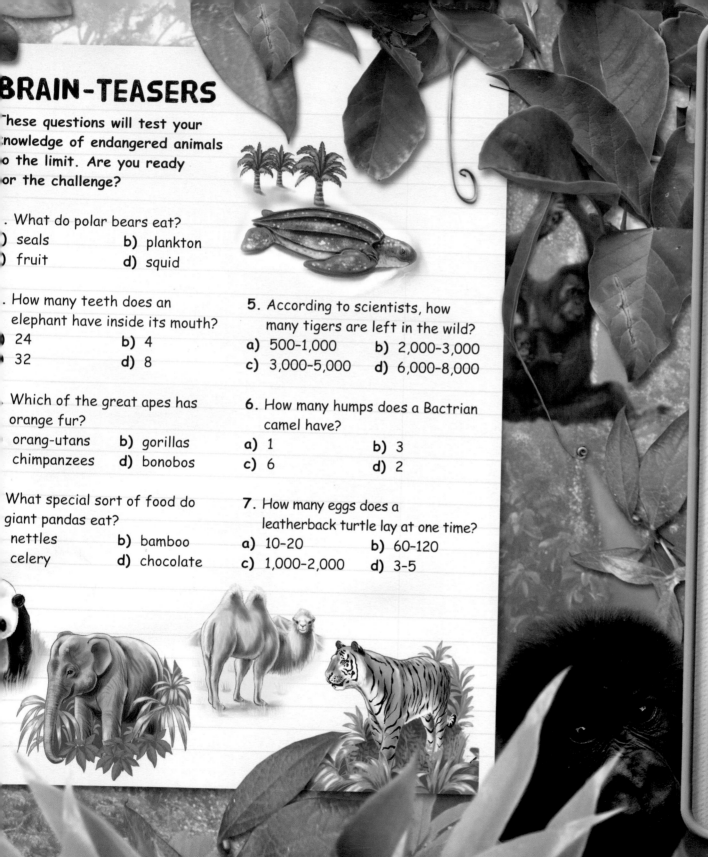

1. What do polar bears eat?
- a) seals
- b) plankton
- c) fruit
- d) squid

2. How many teeth does an elephant have inside its mouth?
- a) 24
- b) 4
- c) 32
- d) 8

3. Which of the great apes has orange fur?
- a) orang-utans
- b) gorillas
- c) chimpanzees
- d) bonobos

4. What special sort of food do giant pandas eat?
- a) nettles
- b) bamboo
- c) celery
- d) chocolate

5. According to scientists, how many tigers are left in the wild?
- a) 500–1,000
- b) 2,000–3,000
- c) 3,000–5,000
- d) 6,000–8,000

6. How many humps does a Bactrian camel have?
- a) 1
- b) 3
- c) 6
- d) 2

7. How many eggs does a leatherback turtle lay at one time?
- a) 10–20
- b) 60–120
- c) 1,000–2,000
- d) 3–5

QUIZ ANSWERS

True or False answers:
1. False. It has over 100 teeth.
2. False. Pandas are always looking for bamboo.
3. False. Rhinos have a very good sense of smell!
4. True. This gives the bears a good grip on the ice.
5. False. The male gorillas are called silverbacks.
6. False. A tiger's fur is striped for camouflage.

Guess who? answers:
1. Orang-utan 2. Camel 3. Panda 4. Tiger 5. Polar bear 6. Panda

Multiple choice answers:
1a 2b 3a 4b 5c 6d 7b

PICTURE CREDITS

The publishers would like to thank the following sources for their kind permission to reproduce the pictures in this book.

Key: t=Top, b=Bottom, c=Centre, l=Left, r=Right, bkgd=Background Image

4-5 (bkgd) Still Pictures/©Klein & Hubert/BIOS; 4bl Panos Pictures/Fred Hoogervorst; 4cb Panos/Tayacan; 5tr Ardea/©Marc Nanzer; 5cb ©NHPA/Martin Harvey; 6-7 (bkgd) naturepl.com/©Staffan Wildstrand; 6 (Cubs) Corbis/©Renee Lynn; 6cl photolibrary.com; 6tr naturepl.com/©Bernard Castelein; 7c Ecoscene/©Satyendra Tiwari; 8-9 (bkgd) FLPA/Frans Lanting; 9tl Corbis/©Momatiuk-Eastcott; 9c photolibrary.com/©Ben Osbourne; 9b Getty/Gianluigi Guercia/AFP; 10-1 (bkgd) naturepl.com/©Toby Sinclair; 10l naturepl.com/©Bernard Castelein; 10br istockphoto.com/Jacques Croizer; 11t Corbis/©Bohemian Nomad Picturemakers; 11bl Alamy Images/©Images of Africa Photobank; 11br photolibrary.com/Mickey Gibson; **Menu:** photolibrary.com/©Zigmund Leszczynski; 12-13 (bkgd) photolibrary.com/©Lynn Stone; 12tr Alamy Images/©Keren Su/China Span; 12bl FLPA/Gerry Ellis/Minden Pictures; 13cl Sinopix; 13cr FLPA/Gerry Ellis/Minden Pictures; 13br (bamboo) NHPA/George Bernard; 14-15 (bkgd) ardea.com/©Charles McDougal; 14bl Jupiter/Nonstock; 14br ardea.com/©Joanna Van Gruisen; 15 (Main Gharial) NHPA/Daniel Heuclin; 15l NHPA/Daniel Heuclin; 15r ardea.com/©Dr.Charles McDougal; 16-17 (Bkgd) naturepl.com/©Huw Cordey; 16bl FLPA/©Mike Lane; 16tr naturepl.com/©Dan Burton; 17 (Main Camel) FLPA/©Fritz Polking; 17t naturepl.com/©Gertrud Helmut Denzau; 17cr naturepl.com/©Huw Cordey; 18-19 (bkgd) FLPA/©Paul Hobson; 18-19 (Foliage) naturepl.com/©Anup Shah; 19 (Main Gorilla) FLPA/©Gerry Ellis/Minden Pictures; 19tr Alamy Images/©Nick Higham; 19br NHPA /Martin Harv; 18br photolibrary.com; 20-21 (bkgd) ardea.com/©M.Watson; 20t FLPA/©Norbert Wu/Minden Pictures; 20b NHPA/©Michael Patrick O'Neill; 21tl NHPA/©Gerald Cubitt; 21tr Alamy/©Visual & Written SL; 21c ardea.com/Masahiro Iijima; 21br FLPA/©Jurgen & Christine Sohns; 21bl NHPA/©Jany Sauvanet; 22l naturepl.com/©Steven Kaziowski; 22r ©istockphoto.com/Stefan Klein; 23c Steve Bloom Images; 23tr FLPA/©Flip Nicklin/Minden Pictures; 23cr naturepl.com/©Steven Kaziowski; 23br istockphoto.com/John Pitcher; 24-25 (bkgd) FLPA/Petra Wallner/Imagebroker; 24bl NHPA/©James Warwick; 24br naturepl.com/©Tony Heald; 25tl Panos Pictures/©Paul Weinberg; 25br Corbis/©Eric Reisinger/Gallo Images; 26-27 (bkgd) FLPA/©Patricio Robles/Sierra Madre/Minden Pictures; 27ct naturepl.com/©Doc White; 27tr FLPA/Flip Nicklin/Minden Pictures; 27tl ardea.com/©Francois Gohier; 27bl Mary Evans Picture Library; 27br photolibrary.com /©Gerald Soury; 28-29 (bkgd) naturepl.com /©Anup Shah; 28 (Main Orangutan) photolibrary.com/©Mike Hill/Osf; 28br FLPA/©Frans Lanting; 29tr FLPA/©ZSSD/Minden Pictures; 29c Ecoscene/Sally Morgan; 29cr FLPA/Frans Lanting; 30-31 (bkgd) FLPA/©Frans Lanting; 30tl FLPA/©ZSSD/Minden Pictures; 30cl Alamy Images/©Keren Su/China Span; 30bl naturepl.com/©Steven Kazlowski; 30tr FLPA/©Mike Lane; 30cr Corbis/©Gallo Images; 30br FLPA/©Gerry Ellis/Minden Pictures; 31t FLPA/©Konrad Wothe/Minden Pictures; 31b FLPA/©Gerry Ellis/Minden Pictures.

Every effort has been made to acknowledge correctly and contact the source and/or copyright holder of each picture and Carlton Books Limited apologizes for any unintentional errors or omissions which will be corrected in future editions of this book.

THE END

THIS IS A CARLTON BOOK

This edition published in 2009

Text and design copyright © Carlton Books Limited 2008
Map illustrations copyright © KJA-Artists 2008
Rhino, gorilla and whale illustrations copyright © County Studio 2008
"How big?" illustrations copyright © Peter Liddiard 2008

First published in 2008 by Carlton Books Limited
An imprint of the Carlton Publishing Group,
20 Mortimer Street, London, W1T 3JW

A catalogue record is available for this book from the British Library.

ISBN: 978-1-84732-325-5

Author: **Barbara Taylor**
Consultant: **Michael Chinery**
Managing editor: **Neil Kelly**
Senior art editor: **Joanne Little**
Development editor: **Selina Wood**

Design: **Jim Lockwood**
Editors: **Bob Bridle, Ben Hoare,
Lara Maiklem**
Picture research: **Jenny Lord**
Production: **Claire Hayward**

Printed and bound in China